FIRE IN THE EARTH

FIRE
IN THE
EARTH

Poems by DAVID WHYTE

FIRE
IN THE
EARTH

Poems by DAVID WHYTE

2 0 0 7

MANY RIVERS PRESS

LANGLEY, WASHINGTON

This book is dedicated to Edward Wates,
a good friend
and a brother in the mountains.

Library of Congress Catalog Card Number 91-066236

1st Printing 1992

2nd Printing 1995

3rd Printing 1997

4th Printing 1999

5th Printing 2002

6th Printing 2007

ISBN 978-0-9621524-2-9

LA POESIA

…And something ignited in my soul,
fever or unremembered wings,
and I went my own way,
deciphering
that burning fire
and I wrote the first bare line,
bare, without substance, pure
foolishness,
pure wisdom
of one who knows nothing,
and suddenly I saw
the heavens
unfastened
and open.

Pablo Neruda   *La Poesia*
                         Trans. D.W.

CONTENTS

CONTENTS *(continued)*

[I]

FIRE IN THE BODY

MILLENNIUM

The years pass quickly
but only frighten
by their speed in the backward view.

These times are times for holding on,
speaking out, stepping carefully
between the broken crystal of a culture

swept from a table filled with too much
for too few. There are no excuses
now and the places left to hide are visible to all.

The glass was broken because it was
broken from the beginning.
The journey begun because the body

takes a step in the first breath.
Wherever we go
we can only take a step from here,

and from wherever we came
we did not come from the place
where the mind waits in safety.

Before humans and as humans
we came from some kind of fire.
The supernova relived in the paint brush

touching cave walls and canvas.
Vision flaring in the hand-held light,
father to son, mother to child.

The fire in the earth first kindling
the flame, the hearth
where we gathered. The center of life

looking out into darkness
made sacred by light.

We needed that center then and shared
our food round that
warming pivot of explosive light.

Now darkness refuses the
periphery, seeping back
along the life lines we used as distance.

Back into the center of safety
where we drew
our sure indignant line of identity.

No one can be ashamed of fear.
Our inheritance is a sense of lack.

And small comfort now
our love of owning
will suddenly not suffice.

Our lives now center on experience
and the fire of its consuming.

Warmed and grown in its light
we prepare our metamorphosis in flame.

Easy the flame of the living death.
Easy the suicidal rush to arms
and the living death-wish of battle.

The way we have gone before.
The way we have rushed to oblivion.
The way we have bargained with life,

giving our life to the wrong life,
hoping many wrong lives consumed
would become as we ate, the one life of desire.

And standing still,
saying I, and the small vision I have
-is enough, becomes the hardest path of all.

The path where we have fallen
refusing to rise again
becomes the spiral line
of flame
where we turn
into the one desire
we have not lived.

The path opens before our eyes
turning into open country,
the wilderness
becomes the path of paths.

Now is the path
of leaving the path.

And we hear our own voice
demanding of ourselves
a faith in no-path,
when there is no faith at all.

And moving forward takes feral courage,
opens the wildest
most outrageous light of all,

becomes the hardest path of all.
The firm line we drew in the sand
becomes a river we will not cross.

But the river of the soul flows on
and the soul
refuses safety until it finds the sea.

The ocean of longing,
the sea of your deeper want,
the gravity well of your own desire,

the place you would fall becomes
in falling
the place you are held.

The great sea
and the still ship of your own
becoming.

But still, on the ocean, there is
no path

only the needle's trembling dance
north

toward the new millennium, followed
without fear,

though the dance now is fear and calmness
in one movement

seeing

as you look
not only at the angry sea
of what you
have denied

but
here,
near at hand,
in the center
of your body,

the rose-fire
of the compass
blossoming
with direction.

FIRE IN THE EARTH

And we know, when Moses was told,
    in the way he was told,
"Take off your shoes!" He grew pale from that simple

reminder of fire in the dusty earth.
    He never recovered
his complicated way of loving again

and was free to love in the same way
    he felt the fire licking at his heels loved him.
As if the lion earth could roar

and take him in one movement.
    Every step he took
from there was carefully placed.

Everything he said mattered as if he knew
    the constant witness of the ground
and remembered his own face in the dust

the moment before revelation.
    Since then thousands have felt
the same immobile tongue with which he tried to speak.

Like the moment you too saw, for the first time,
    your own house turned to ashes.
Everything consumed so the road could open again.

Your entire presence in your eyes
    and the world turning slowly
into a single branch of flame.

WHAT IT MEANS TO BE FREE

We sit on the plane, we watch,
we see clouds, grey hills,
the road edged with fuschia,
and from a vision, near Bantry,
an old man walking on the wet road.

Behind him the light opens
in an long arch across the sea.
He has a stick, a hat, old shoes,
a gait that says he will walk forever.

He reaches out, touching the bright
bell-like overhanging flowers with his stick.
His face lifts, catching the light as I look
out the window through deep veils
of cynicism and irony flooding the landscape.

From his face I look down at my book
into the dark interior of the plane
surprised by the single tear.
Knowing how long it took - even to feel.
Now its seems after years of walking
the homecoming happened in a single step.

The imagination cradled so long
returns grown with its manly gift
and the shut bud of my emotion
opens like a flower on the white page.

SELF-PORTRAIT

It doesn't interest me if there is one God
or many gods.
I want to know if you belong or feel
abandoned.
If you can know despair or see it in others.
I want to know
if you are prepared to live in the world
with its harsh need
to change you. If you can look back
with firm eyes
saying this is where I stand. I want to know
if you know
how to melt into that fierce heat of living
falling toward
the center of your longing. I want to know
if you are willing
to live, day by day, with the consequence of love
and the bitter
unwanted passion of your sure defeat.

I have heard, in *that* fierce embrace, even
the gods speak of God.

WAITING ON THE STEPPES

What was that dream?
Year after year I knew
the brief, cloud-lit heaven of
its quiet visitation.

The railway platform
in the silence of a summer day,
the tracks closing quietly
to a middle distance
of golden wheat
and beyond that
a deeper gold,
the three domes of a far
Kremlin, shimmering like a mirage,
as if beckoning, as if,
to my clear child's eye
a place I could know again,
a bright sun of welcome,
a treasure house of pure home.

My presence there
a sure kind of stillness,
stillness born of the waiting
as if the body
I possessed
was neither young nor old
but flamed with a longing
and a harvest
as rich as the fields themselves.

In that waiting was another pure silence
and in that silence
a deeper waiting yet
sure in the knowledge of the train
that would arrive,
its patience
and power endless
its destination clear.

But looking back,
I know you'll say,
that not having dreamt for years
these lines invoke the grief
we share in growing old.

You feel experience
must mean forgetting,
vision must mean regret,
longing spells
disappointment
and desire speaks
only of shame.

And Russia
is not the place
it could have been.

Only sometimes
out of nowhere
the last smoulder
of an old wish
kindles
our accumulated fear
and we rise in the flame again.

The gold no longer pure
and the vision blurred.
But then
being blind and poor
we find another peace
and learn to wait again
in that place
where longing is the gold that flares
and waiting can be its own sun
and forgiveness
its own far dome
of belonging,
a vast Russia of the possible
longing for itself again
in the intimate patience
of your new body.

TRAVELING TO LONDON

Coleridge's eyes
belonged to the world.
The black mass
of starlings
smoking over the ridge
was his life.
No fancy this
but feverish
with their black shapes
his view
was to fly with them.
Make each word
follow each bird.
His grief accorded
directly
from what he saw
but could not speak.
Their mesmerizing dispersion
summed up the
limit of his powers.
Their protean shape
shifting through
his jolted body
held joy and chaotic
terror
as if he glimpsed
through the moving
carriage window
a portrait of himself
too terrifying to realize.

Now, the wintry
line of moor glowering
to an unnamed blue
broods beneath
an empty grey.
Now, each black speck
scattered and reformed
holds attention
to its gravitational
center. The turbulent
reflector of his eyes
no longer accustomed
to watching can only
join its misted surface
of infinitely smaller
curves. Beneath,
the graph-straight line
of the moors
where imagination
equals zero,
is cut again and again
by their flight.

The flight of amazing freedoms
held in tension
by the menace
of impending chaos.

The cloud
of his own unknowing
darting this way
and that.

Like the lithe
shadow
of something deeper
suddenly revealed
in the sky.
His single vision
exploded
to a firework of doubles.

THE ELDERSHIP OF PRAISE

Wordsworth's body
was a slow turn
in a great river
feeling its way
to a distant sea.

His child's eyes
accustomed to loss
grew strong
in their aloneness,
taught him to feel
the terrible weight
and onward flow
of things
as joy.

His own blood
moved like that river
alive to the slow
inward turn of attention,
the soil
of the mountains
on their way
to the sea,
filling
the estuaries of his own
desire,
branching
into the dark
invisible
workmanship of his first
belonging.

Our age
mistrusts his balance
demands, if not a saint,
a devil
to make our weakness
right.
He knew
his own doubt
and saw the dawn
in which he came alive
clouded by fear
but found
doubt's door
led back
into the world,
and lived
to see it
flower
into a larger
sun.
Suckled in his outworn
creed
he saw a desert
but grew
larger with that thirst,
saw the dark
subterranean
stream of natural revelation
rising to the surface
and brought us
to the spring to drink.

We lived in those
islands
a thousand years
without
the eldership of praise
for what is hidden
in the woods,
the water,
land and sky
until the long chant
of his song
began to move
our lips again.

THE PAINTER'S HAND

You start
with a painter's hand
working up color
from a dark palette
of remembrance.

It used to be guess-work
touching the pigments
as if they might at any point
betray the startling vision
of its need to live.

Now the paint itself startles
and the hand darting
to the blank canvas
returns the color whole
to the remembered world
from which it came.

Wrong touches
make the blood freeze
a moment before contact.

A color's deepening field
of visual gravity's
deflected a moment before
it pulls the image down.

The fierce eye
of remembrance
finding the eye
of eternal presence
absolves
the mind
of its struggle to live.

The blaze of yellow
Vincent
mistook for God
reveals again
its sacred name.

The light from the window
traveling home
becomes
in the flattened brush
a journey
complete.

Now something
outside the window
high in the branches
of the fiery trees
announces that other
hidden and unseeable
name of light
falling onto
the stretched canvas
where my hand moves
firmly.

The artist gladly resigns
his freedom
in the split second
when the hand feels the brush
halt on the painting's
opening world.

The lost world
where we live
and remember
not wishing freedom
for a moment.

THIS TIME

This time he has gone
too far.
The chair overturned
on the floor,
the accusation, the door
banging wildly.
He will not return. Everything
he has gained
he is willing to lose.
Is glad to lose.

Because he loved too much
his own redemption.
Because he felt
he could not be touched.
Because he hoped
he would not need that touch.
He is willing to go
where he should not go.

The night is familiar.
The wind is cold.
He has no future,
only the words
"I will not go back."

As the road steepens,
his grief goes ahead,
reaches the top,
turns round, watches him
with the dead child's face.
This is not to be spoken of.

He stopped,
"I will not go back"
trembled through his body.

He did not go back.
He stood, mouth open,
watching the lonely stars
rise from darkness.
He listened. He heard
for the first time
the clear grief of his voice.
He leant against the wall.
He wept. He felt his breath
rising and falling.
Dead already
he had nothing to lose.
He stood up and wavered,
the faint stars glimmering.
A strange dignity
in his bowed head.
A broken man
holding the ashes
of an only child.

He felt himself cradled
by strong arms.
He opened his eyes
in those arms
and saw the stars.

Those stars told him
they loved him only
for what *he* loved himself.
They did not love him
for what he was.

From the dark town
A bell chimed
"Nowhere to go."
A half promise from
the half-killed dream
of his life.
He was the other half.

Something was happening.
Somewhere in the high tower
of the long night
the bell went on chiming.
Destroyed, lost, killed,
but finally, in this new presence
surviving. He would not go back.
He would not go on.

NEVER ENOUGH

It is never enough. The three riders
arrive with gifts. The woman brings food.
The child looks with admiring eyes.

Something else is triggered. He hears
unaccountably the voice of someone he knew.
He pulls back the curtain. No one.
At night he opens his depths
and dreams. He will not appear.
He turns to the old part of himself
known since a boy. Gone.
The door open in the night wind
and on the oak table a note.
"I am to be trusted but you are not".

He remembers everything he can. His face.
His hands. The way he would rise as if to speak.
Oblivion begins to pull on its long shroud.
He has one moment before panic.
His voice ready to pounce on death
unsheathes its secret claws. His hour.
His place. His voice with its new sound.
A bunched animal cornered by stealth.

Then someone gets up, closes the door,
begins to speak.

YOU DARKNESS

You darkness from which I come,
I love you more than all the fires
that fence out the world,
for the fire makes a circle
for everyone
so that no one sees you anymore.

But darkness holds it all:
the shape and the flame,
the animal and myself,
how it holds them,
all powers, all sight-

and it is possible: its great strength
is breaking into my body.

I have faith in the night.

Rainer Maria Rilke   *Trans. D.W.*

[II]

FIRE IN THE VOICE

THE SOUL LIVES CONTENTED

The soul lives contented
by listening,
if it wants to change
into the beauty of
terrifying shapes,
it tries to speak.

That's why
you will not sing,
afraid as you are
of who might join with you.

The voice hesitant,
and her hand trembling
in the dark for yours.

She touches your face
and says your name
in the same moment.

The one you refused to say,
over and over,
the one you refused to say.

REVELATION MUST BE TERRIBLE

Revelation must be
  terrible with no time left
to say goodbye.

Imagine that moment
  staring at the still waters
with only the brief tremor

of your body to say
  you are leaving everything
and everyone you know behind.

Being far from home is hard, but you know,
  at least we are all exiled together.
When you open your eyes to the world

you are on your own for
  the first time. No one is
even interested in saving you now

and the world steps in
  to test the calm fluidity of your body
from moment to moment

as if it believed you could join
  its vibrant dance
of fire and calmness and final stillness.

As if you were meant to be exactly
   where you are, as if
like the dark branch of a desert river

you could flow on without a speck
   of guilt and everything
everywhere would still be just as it should be.

As if your place in the world mattered
   and the world could
neither speak nor hear the fullness of

its own bitter and beautiful cry
   without the deep well
of your body resonating in the echo.

Knowing that it takes only
   that one, terrible
word to make the circle complete,

revelation must be terrible
   knowing you can
never hide your voice again.

IN THE BEGINNING

Sometimes simplicity rises
　　like a blossom of fire
　　　　from the white silk of your own skin.

You were there in the beginning
　　you heard the story, you heard the merciless
　　　　and tender words telling you where you had to go.

Exile is never easy and the journey
　　itself leaves a bitter taste. But then,
　　　　when you heard that voice, you had to go.

You couldn't stay by the fire, you couldn't live
　　so close to the live flame of that compassion
　　　　you had to go out in the world and make it your own

so you could come back with
　　that flame in your voice, saying listen...
　　　　this warmth, this unbearable light, this fearful love...

It is all here, it is all here.

THE FIRE IN THE SONG

The mouth opens
  and fills the air
    with its vibrant shape

until the air
  and the mouth
    become one shape.

And the first word,
  your own word,
    spoken from that fire

surprises, burns,
  grieves you now
    because

you made that pact
  with a dark presence
    in your life.

He said, "If you only
  stop singing
    I'll make you safe."

And he repeated the line,
  knowing you would hear
    "I'll make you safe"

as the comforting
  sound of a door
    closed on the fear at last,

but his darkness crept
  under your tongue
    and became the dim

cave where
  you sheltered
    and you grew

in that small place
  too frightened to remember
    the songs of the world,

its impossible notes,
  and the sweet joy
    that flew out the door

of your wild mouth
  as you spoke.

THE CAREFUL STONE OF MY VOICE

Someone once told me
in secret
that under
the carefully placed stone
of my voice
lay a gift.

I lay still
like that stone
not daring
to move.

The child spent
hours down by the sea
turning those green
stones toward the sun.

But one day grew afraid.

This is a familiar story
one you've
grown tired of telling.

And fear begins to
settle now in the deep well
of your throat.

Like a stone
falling away from you.
The same stone
that fills your mouth
when you try to speak.

As if the stone
becomes you.
And trying
to speak from its cold center
you become
the coldness yourself.

And you hear it
when you try to say
the one word
that makes a difference in your life.

But the stone awaits
you in another way.
Its weight adds firmness now
and coldness only sharpens you to feel
the harsh presence of
an old love you refused.

In the center of the stone
there is a diamond
which is never brought to light.

Even when the darkness is filled
with that light
it still remains dark.

This is a mercy.
It cannot be given away.

Now, in one instant,
give me your word

and keep it.

THE SOUND OF THE WILD

Finally
at the first firm
shadow
of evening
and
after many hours
falling toward
the body's
ebb and flow
of quiet revelation,

I hear that
voice
which belongs
to no one
except
the hidden
world
from which it flows
like a river
filling the deep branches
of my body
with the wish to
slip beneath its quiet water
and disappear,

and listening
in the half light
beneath the
sound
of a single
brooding dove

I try
to remember
my former life

and realize how quickly
the current travels
toward home

how those
dark and irretrievable
blossoms of sound
I made in that time
have traveled
far-away
on the black surface
of memory

as if they no longer
belonged
to me.

As if my body might
feel lighter
without
their
weight
on what I have to say.

All night I followed
those currents
down to the sea
and finally
with that sweet
entangled
encouragement
we get
from greeting everything
we meet
along the way
as if we might
belong,

I sacrificed at the shores
of that great silence
my last possibility
for safety.

That's why I speak
the way I do.
I'm like everything else,
I have no immunity.

That's a fearful thing
to say
and having been there
you'll know
how much it means.

-We humans must be
such strange
and reluctant
creatures to live with.

All those cries
in the night
with which we could join,
the fox
crying *fox*

and those winged
and silent creatures
of the dusk

dropping with
such fierce delicacy
onto the shrew's
tremulous back.

Even when the owl
is silent
the shrew cries *owl*
into the black woods
its life a last blaze
of sound
before the
small fire of its body
goes out.

Our own sounds
we refuse,
terrified as we are
to wake that voice
inside us
waiting
with its wings folded
and its strange
expectant face.

The moment we try
to explain ourselves
he moves those wings
to cover his face

and longs for
the wild
where cries
are involuntary things

and everybody
generously
gives their voice
to others
even in their
last breath.

But this can be
no comfort,

knowing
the world
learns
the sound of its
own name
by dropping its
fearful weight
on us
out of the dark
when we least
expect,

so we can know the full
terror
of that love,

like the shrew
shrieking
its final gift-*owl!*

THE HUSK OF YOUR VOICE

The husk of your voice
is like a chrysalis
grown round something
hidden,
waiting to be born
and waiting for you
to stop.

What is inside
wants you to know itself fully
before it is born.

That's why it refuses
to reveal itself,
sure as you are
that you need not slip down
that long branch of your body
to the very root
and in that earth
hear the damp echo
of everything
you have not touched
reflected
in your voice, and the air
suddenly quicken

as if innocent speech
could rise again
from that rich and
impossible soil
composed
of your neglected
past.

Like sap rising
in the steady tree
of your life.

Your voice opens
and shows
the strong outline
of that tree
against the sky,

where another
shadow
takes flight
startled by your
new cry,

the shadow
of something leaving
to find its own way
in the world.

Something you carried
as a black weight
for many years.

You watch it go
relieved
as if it might return
blessed by a world
which
allows its going,
refusing to be held
and refusing to hold
you again,
free and finally
in its flight
to another's mouth
untroubled by your breath.

THE POET

moves forward
to that edge
but lives sensibly,

through the senses
not because of them.

Above all he watches
where he steps.
As if it matters
where he leaves his prints.

The senses overwhelm him
at his peril.

Though he *must* be taken
by something greater.
That is what he uses
senses to perceive.

The poet's

task is simple.
He looks for quiet,
and speaks to what
he finds there.

But like Blake
in his engraving shop, works
with the fierceness
of acid on metal.

Melting away apparent
surfaces and displaying
the infinite
which was hid.

In the early morning
he listens
by the window,
makes
the first utterance
and tries to overhear
himself
say something
from which
in that silence
it is impossible to retreat.

THE BODY IN FULL PRESENCE

The body in full presence
holds its first creative essence
in the pen that touches paper.
Lifting the glass that holds the wine
this beckoning uncertainty is mine.

I'll follow my line to an early death,
feeling out rhythm in the spoken breath
and startled by flame
this arrogance shall be my moth
flying with his burning cloth.

And humility will rise
out of poetry's deep surmise.
Then, I have confidence in my powers,
and wanting this presence, burnt by the past,
I'll die in the first line - and become the last.

NO ONE TOLD ME

No one told me
it would lead to this.
No one said
there would be secrets
I would not want to know.

No one told me about seeing,
seeing brought me
loss and a darkness I could not hold.

No one told me about writing
or speaking.
Speaking and writing poetry
I unsheathed the sharp edge
of experience that led me here.

No one told me
it could not be put away.
I was told once, only,
in a whisper,
"The blade is so sharp-
It cuts things together
-not apart."

This is no comfort.
My future is full of blood
from being blindfold
hands outstretched,
feeling a way along its firm edge.

HORSE IN LANDSCAPE: FRANZ MARC

We know the fiery animality
of the purebred horse,
its ghostly hide moving like smoke
over the green landscape.

But must remember
in that wild vulnerability
a natural power of rest.

Marc did it with a bold gesture.
Painted the neck
rising to the curved horizon
and its blue mane swelling in waves.

Primary colors and prime emotion
swirl in the coiled flank.
Head rearing to the pasture's expanse.

The landscape living in its body
as the sinewy horse lives in the world.

Now, as it turns toward you,
head curved to one side
and the wild mane flying
above the distant hoof beats'
incantatory silence,
you are asked again —

What will you do
and what will you say
in the times
when you are left alone
to meet, like this,
the quiet fury of the world?

SECOND BIRTH

The wild dream, two whirling lights
turned one inside the other
and then away. The child's terror
seeing one as his mother,
and that black space opened into nothing
the hand outstretched
toward the perfect ring
of light becoming other.

And I, after the first birth
and that first unspeaking error
will undertake a second birth
and so relinquish terror.

THE OLD WILD PLACE

After the good earth
where the body knows itself to be real
and the mad flight
where it gives itself to the world,
we give ourselves to the rhythm of love
leaving the breath
to know its way home.

And after the first pure fall,
the last letting go, and the calm
breath where we go to rest,
we'll return again to find it
and feel again the body welcomed
the body held,
the strong arms of the world,
the water, the waking at dawn
and the thankful, almost forgotten,
curling to sleep with the dark.

The old wild place beyond all shame.

UNUTTERABLE NAME

Cross-currents and tumbling desire
of aspens in a summer wind,
shimmering in a rustle and whisper

of leaf undersides turned pale
yellow, each upper side
a trembling of bright greeñ.

The whole frame a lit firework
of feeling where all
surfaces and shoulders of wood

and leaf touch and quiver
to the wind's
quaking unspoken desire.

Not to be lightly spoken of.
Your species name
so common on our tongue

the mind's eye forgets the continued
revelation of your kind.
A single branch, a copse, a nest of bright

copper for the dying year. All the
forests of the world
were wild wood once and proclaim

the leafy hope and snares of human paradise.
The wild wood, bramble, columbine,
the oak tree's deciduous stability of half-light.

In your branches the robin and the wren,
the crows, the rooks, the owls, the sparrow-
hawk gliding the fine speckled corridors of light.

Of all your many worlds I'll start by naming home,
this sharp evergreen night's
rough-barked verticality of totem and grey wood

lifted two hundred feet to a cold sky,
its grey clouds unseen above the world's
green turn of pine and hemlock, fir and cedar

shadowing the padded needle beds
in their brown sleep.
Even here, Pan's mad flute wakes them all,

a scurry of chipmunks and tremulous mice,
a moment's panic before the
creaking whine of a branch lifts the hair

straight on the neck, the owl's prey screams
in discovered claws and the patient empty
darkness of the deep wood returns to quiet.

Even then, the still temple of the northern night
opening its doors to the first delicate light
and the nightjar burring at a branch edge

is nothing to the jungle's southern tumult and tropic
dark panoply of explosive sound.
In that equatorial fusion of heat and noise,

where a scream would be lost in the whistling,
cawing, shuddering, sighing
rippling, spider-monkeyed laugh and great shaking

of the canopy's jungle dark essence,
there lies that eternally moving
half-hidden, essentially frightening

forest of our own inner night. Down below,
the dream of those dark limbs turning
now feminine, now snake-like, erotically

refusing to be found, leads us down
into that glistering world-wide
treasure of wetness and wild abandon, the marsh.

The dank water's cool refusal of dryness
a sworn enemy to the clarity
our yearning demands, every footstep

filled with mud, every feeling a mere mushroom
subsumed by damp, a fever
of scents, sounds and recollection, how the bark

smells, how the frogs breathe, how the greens
seem darker still. How the faint
brushing sting of nettle feels on passing skin.

The stagnant still fullness of it all with no place
to rest, sit, camp, cook, build,
get in, get out, lie down with self or other.

The infuriating self-satisfied independent
non-human presence
of this methane-flitted, black and fiery

incandescence of wetness eschewing our praise,
resting into its own eternal wet grave
of damp hidden mischief. The damned and lovely swamp.

Not forgetting for one moment the dry desert
branches of the world's
desiccated, rough-barked, wax-leafed elders.

The pinon, chaparral, boll-weed and wind-dried
dust-loving Joshua, even the names
have a dry mouth salted by heat and smothered

by thirst. Tenacity a prize of their kind,
living patiently through the hard
baked inhospitable prison of eternal summer,

and they need, we still do not believe it,
just the one, gifted, single drop
of fecund rain swimming through red earth

to break out in a blood red, snow white
festival of still flowers.
Or a lit inextinguishable fire of perfect yellow.

All your many kinds are filled with our stories.
We know you, name you
Aspen, Rowan, Linden, Oak, and remember

Pan's stable of haunting desire,
Kevin's seat of still prayer,
Buddha's explosive clarity beneath

the Bodhi's protecting shadow of knowledge.
Christ's arms like branches
on the still sapling of longing and loss.

Your stories are our welcome night sign
of stop and rest and sky and stars
and forgotten sleep where we wake again

to find we are surrounded, embellished,
frighted, nourished,
sheltered, restored, rejected and inhabited

by - how shall I ever say your name?
Wood, trunk, branch, leaf,
boreal harmony of green in-breath,

my hands clapping, eyes opened,
mouth attempting the song
of your unspeakable gifts and grace

again and again- the full hidden
not to be said, mysterious
and unutterable name of your full breath. Tree.

[III]

FIRE IN THE QUIET

SITTING ZEN

After three days of sitting
hard by the window
following grief through
the breath

like a hunter
who has tracked for days
the blood spots
of his injured prey

I came to the lake
where the deer had run
exhausted

refusing to save
its life in the
dark water

and there it fell
to ground
in our mutual
and respectful quiet

pierced
by
the pale diamond
edge of the breath's
listening
presence.

AGAIN

All those
gone before me
sit with me now.

The line
of the sun's shadow
edging on the far line of trees.

The readiness
to hear, sing, see,
the flowering of everything

I was afraid to
say, being said, without
fear or unnecessary words,

at rest
in the field
of the possible

and the
secret that could
not be spoken again,

again . . .

Without
the least need
to say anything.

IMAGINE MY SURPRISE

Imagine my surprise,
sitting a full hour
in silent and irremediable
fear of the world,

to find the body
forgetting
its own fear the instant
it opened and placed
those unassuming hands
on life's enduring pain,

and the world for one
moment
closed its terrifying eyes
in gratitude.

Saying.
"This is my body, I am found."

OPEN

It is a small step to remember
how life led to this
moment's hesitation.

How the door to the deeper world
opens, letting the body fall at last,
toward the few griefs it can call its own.

Oh yes, I know. Our wings catch fire
in that downward flight
and we come to earth afraid
we can never fly again.

But then we always knew
heaven would be a desperate place.
Everything you desired coming
in one fearful moment
to greet you.

Your full presence only in rest
and the love that asks nothing.
The rest where you lie down
and are no longer found at all.

WE SHALL NOT BE HERE

Heaven has been
promised
in great detail.

Beyond this silence
we shall not be here
to find it.
And that, my friend

is a great joy.

DEATH WAITS

Death waits behind the branches
refusing to show his face.

The child opens his eyes and sees
the delicate leaves

swaying in the light wind that
touches his own face.

Life moves just beyond the limit
of our powers

having shown us in the moonlight
her whole body.

I remember
needing nothing

but what I could smell and touch
and hear in the minute

eternity between sounds or the long
shimmer of the barley's

green-gold dance on the wind.
My life a spreading ring

of quiet, like the trout's brief
in-breath

at the surface of a river,
like the slow

outward movement of a raindrop
spreading on a still lake.

Like the silence in which I opened my eyes
to that shadow

behind the branch, to see his half-turned
face for a moment

and heard the church tower belling
a slow sound

through white mist, tolling my new
and terrible maturity.

MIDSUMMER PRAYER

In midsummer, under the luminous
sky of everlasting light,

the laced structures of thought
fall away

like the filigrees of the white
diaphanous

dandelion turned pure white and
ghostly,

hovering at the edge of its own
insubstantial

discovery in flight. I'll do the same,
watch

the shimmering dispersal of tented
seeds

lodge in the tangled landscape
without

the least discrimination. So let my own
hopes

escape the burning wreck of ambition,
parachute

through the hushed air, let them spread
elsewhere,

into the tangled part of life that refuses
to be set straight.

Herod searched for days looking for
the children.

The mind's hunger for fame will hunt down
all innocence.

Let them find safety in the growing wild.
I'll not touch them there.

THE HALF TURN OF YOUR FACE

The half turn of your face
toward truth
is the one movement
you will not make.

After all,
having seen it
before,

you wouldn't
want
to take that
path again,

and have to greet
yourself
as you are
and tell yourself
what it was like
to have come so far
and all in vain.

But most of all
to remember
how it felt again
to see
reflected
in your own mirror,
the lines
of abandonment
and loss.

And have those words spoken
inviting you back,
the ones you used to say,
the ones you loved
when your body was young
and you trusted
everything you wanted.

Hard to look,
but you know it has to happen
and
that it takes
only the half turn of your face
to scare yourself
to the core.
Seeing again
that strange resolve in your new reflection.

[IV]

FIRE IN THE MOUNTAINS

THIS POEM A PRAYER FLAG

This poem a prayer flag.
Almost written, then gone.
The wind–I cannot touch it!

TAKSTANG

Takstang monastery,
the tiger's nest.

Two thousand feet
to the valley floor.

After many days
alone in the mountains

the body hesitates
at the sight of a single roof.

Having listened to the wind,
sufficient to itself

like a single clear breath
from the body of the mountain,

we hear the sutra's
diamond hard presence

at the center of experience
so clearly now,

spoken from the felt rhythm
of a ten-day walk.

And having crossed the pass
in cold rain

we wait, about to ripen
into our own going.

Like a drop of clear water
hanging from the cliff edge,

its own transparent world
growing from within,

until it fills with just enough
to flow on

out of the mountains
as we do.

So silent now, only the sound,
as we go

of that pure water
falling

toward home.

MOUNTAIN FEVER

The Black Tent
of the nomad family
shrouds their
watchful daughter.

Seeing me so close
she calls back
into the tent
and I see them appear,
black as their rough dwelling.

Their faces encrusted
with wood smoke
and lined by the keen wind
they watch me take
the narrow
cliff-edged path
toward Lingshi.

Walking alone
I feel thin beads of sweat
running on my forehead
and the feverish heat
of chill wind
on my cheek.

Since the crest of Nyele La
and the first
pulse of weakness,
this fire in the body
continues to burn.

I walk ahead
to get down quickly,
but only keep up
with the yak-train
until the meadows widen
and they begin to run,
the yak-boys following,
singing
encouragement.

And walking in the
hallucinatory rhythm
of the entranced,
I hear my pulse like
a steady incantation,
secret, chanted,
close to the ear,
while the yak songs
fade in a delirious
middle distance.

A Blue-headed
Redstart,
its startled call
an emblem
for my inflamed
hearing, flicks its tail
in danger,
tells me of the
hawk-shadow
floating above.

Over the great while
barrier guarding Tibet
the Himalayan Griffon
has held me all day.

His keen eye
following
this slight stumble
in my walk.

Is it our weakness
makes us belong?
This shadow told me it was.
His presence
so much attentive grace
gliding with me
through that feverish haze.

My feet
needed strength
for only the first step
toward home,
the world did the rest.

The perfect discriminating
mind unable to choose
one thing calls
on the flawed heart
to reveal them all.

Beneath me, floating on mist,
the fortress
monastery
of Lingshi Dzong
a white ship,
with red sails
framed by a rainbow.

THE OLD INTERIOR ANGEL

Young, male and
immortal as I was,
I stopped at the first sight
of that broken bridge.

The taut cables snapped
and the bridge planks
concertina-ed
into a crazy jumble
over the drop,
four hundred feet
to the craggy
stream.

I sat and watched
the wind shiver
on the broken planks,
as if by looking hard
and long enough
the life-line
might spontaneously
repair itself
-but watched in vain.

An hour I sat
in silence,
checking each
involuntary movement
of the body toward
that trembling
bridge
with a fearful mind,
and an emphatic
shake of the head.

Finally, facing defeat
and about to go back
the way I came
to meet the others.

Three days round
by another pass.

Enter the old mountain woman
with her stooped gait,
her dark clothes
and her dung basket
clasped to her back.

Small feet shuffling
for the precious
gold-brown
fuel for cooking food.

Intent on the ground
she glimpsed my feet
and looking up
Said "Namaste"
"I greet the God in you"
the last syllable
held like a song.

I inclined my head
and clasped my hands
to reply, but
before I could look up
she turned her lined face
and went straight across
that shivering chaos
of wood
and broken steel
in one movement.

One day the hero
sits down,
afraid to take
another step,
and the old interior angel
limps slowly in
with her no-nonsense
compassion
and her old secret
and goes ahead.

"Namaste"
you say
and follow.

STATUE OF BUDDHA

Your hand moves
in the gesture of welcome.
Your lips in the gestures of praise.

You believed in your own sound
and so everything you said
is still being spoken.

In that first step
away from home
you came so far, and all alone,
faithful to all things
as you met them
until finally everything
bowed to you
and everything spoke to you
in its own voice.

You were the child
whose first step
encompassed the four directions.
You said,
"Heaven above, earth below,
I alone and sacred".

Creation means
finding the new world
in that first
fierce step,
with no thought of return.

THE STATUE OF SHIVA

The statue of Shiva
entwined with his lover
- the way
we love to hold closely
what is ours.

Their speech
so plain to the attentive ear
bowing close to listen.

"The universe refuses the vows
of the celibate.
Preparing them instead with
songs for marriage.
Everything it knows
was born of the great embrace."

HERE IN THE MOUNTAINS

There is one memory deep inside you.
In the dark country of your life
it is a small fire burning forever.

Even after all these years
of neglect
the embers of what you have
known rest contented
in their own warmth.

Here in the mountains,
tell me all the things
you have not loved.
Their shadows will tell you
they have not gone,
they became this night
from which you drew away in fear.

Though at the trail's end,
your heart stammers
with grief and regret,
in this
final night
you will lean down at last
and breathe again on the
small campfire of your
only becoming.

And draw about you
the immensity
of the black sky
which loves your fire's
centrality.

The deep shadow
that forever
takes
you in its arms.

The low song
of the long
and patient night
that holds you
in your sleep

and stitches
faithfully
with that impossible light
the dark blanket
from which you were born.

David Whyte grew up among the hills and valleys of Yorkshire, England; moved to higher ground in the mountains of Wales, traveled the world, and now lives at sea-level on Whidbey Island, Washington with his son, Brendan.

Fire in the Earth is one of four books of poetry by David Whyte, the others being *Songs for Coming Home, Where Many Rivers Meet,* and *The House of Belonging.* He is the author of two best-selling books of prose, *The Heart Aroused: Poetry and the Preservation of the Soul in Corporate America,* and *Crossing the Unknown Sea: Work as a Pilgrimage of Identity,* and a highly acclaimed audio lecture series, available from bookstores or directly from Many Rivers Press at (360) 221-1324.

www.davidwhyte.com